The Sunrise's Commandment

Lamine Pearlheart

ISBN - 978-1-9995751-0-6

OTHER BOOKS BY THE SAME AUTHOR

To Life from the Shadows

The Sunrise Scrolls

The Mayan Twins - At the Edge of Xibalba's Well

Aether

PREFACE

In this book, you will find mistakes, but they are mine,

You will see a shadow, the one I am attempting to surpass and the one you perhaps have surpassed or do attempt to leave behind,

You will see thoughts trying to rise from the distant future into the present,

You will find you and I for we know not who we are,

You will find one succinct and elusive commandment, which may have been staring at you your entire life,

Idle not, for to you are opened the gates of a distant mind

Table of Contents

To Life,

The Spark

It rises from the depth of despair
It finds reasons where reasons seek none

It soothes the rocks with the soft touch of the waves
It lingers in the dark and hides in the light
It is not a stranger to the fool and sage

It dances in the summits and it twirls on the surface of the abyss
If you find her, you find her

The moon finds her in the day
The sun waits for her in the night

She is the only view, and she points at you

You can see it in the birds floating in the air
In the dolphins flying across the waves gracing the sails

All singing the same tune

It greets the angry volcano seeking a friend in the solitude of the oceans,
It wraps a blanket of green around its fields of desiccated grounds
No longer lonely as its roots extends to the other side of a floating land,
They embrace each other with vibrating sounds,
A venture of two projections in time beyond the common tally and age of humankind

Kind, it is to the muse as it unfurls the sails of the mind

To see beyond the deftness of anger, vengeance and pride
As the roar of the lions fade, devoured by the depth of the solid ground

Finding the reflection and recognizing the sameness of intent,
To wait like the earth awaits the sun,
A curve of attraction between two evidently common, yet extraordinary objects

A dance and a certitude of being one
The promise of light is to attempt and reach the farthest and darkest nights

The promise of love is to keep a heartbeat for as long as a heart knows how to beat

To follow the two in the exactitude of one

To know that which the two only know

The palm trees giving the desert, the beach, the lonely island their token of burst of life
A propulsion of potential of all that is and could become

Life, a particle in all and one
No contradiction, but logic sound

Gravity pulled by its weight clinging to infinite space
The void filled by invisible ropes dancing to the tune of humanity's imagination

Pebbles of rocks in the emptiness of the universe
A beautiful world for fools who refuse to see

It lingers in the dark and hides in the light
It is not a stranger to the fool and sage

If you find her you find me

On Rebirth

They saw it fade, felt sorry for its parting, and as it was leaving it said, "it is alright, for I am reborn in myself."

I did not know how it came about, but the others called it the Sun.

On Your Mind

Let your mind dance to its own rhymes like the children dance without music but to the rhythm of their own imagination. They borrow none from others.

This is how you were meant to think before you were intoxicated.

On Hate as a Seed

"You must hate me?" The offending soul asked. "No, I was frustrated with you, to hate you means that I have let you plant some of your essence into my inner self; I do not do that. You were an objection, but now I can see beyond your insignificance." Said I.

If Evil...

If evil reaches your body, don't let it access your spirit. Otherwise, it will win

If it gazes into your spirit, show it your brave heart made of steel

And if it attempts to dominate it, show it the certainty of your soul and it will run away like a coward, because it does not have one; to have courage one must have a soul

And if by subterfuge it chooses love to scare you, tell it that you are for real; hate, you leave it to the blind; those who do not want to see

You, you are made of concrete there where the hearts are made of hay
You are solitude facing the inevitable ruin of the herd

If it tries to intimidate you through fear, remember that its means define it
Show it its earthworm beginnings, the closest way to its reverse

You do not have to be a human being to be as dumb
You do not have to become dumb to prove that you are a human being

The tomb that buries the living is sometimes mistakenly called life because the excuse of every crime is abandonment

The reverse of death is life

Remember that the first one is also defined by its means

Life is not a banner
It needs no permission to exist

Its state of being is vivid
Its perfume is all that is not livid

Her glory? She does not have any

It vibrates without the need of affirming courtesans
It sows its magic under the nose of the clueless busy artisans
Just as well as on the thundering expanse of the volcanoes

It is as discreet as the rays of the sun
As true and brave as honesty facing a loaded gun

Find her gaze and you will find your soul as it surprises you

On Loud Ranting

A man who shares his personal frustrations out loud with the world, does he want or expect the world to carry it for him?

Doesn't he realize that the world has carried him so far?

On Bravery

You are brave, you faced death, I hand it to you, but have you faced life?

You and Your Shadow

All your life you have been either in front or behind your shadow, now you become one. - *On death*

A Corporate Commandment

"Thou shalt have liberty, but no will."

Lest You,

Lest you think them brave, I point to their nightmares

Lest you believe them rich, I point to their finality in time

Lest you are impressed by their demeanour, I call unto you their thirst for recognition

Lest you think them bright, I point to their stuttering ideas

Lest you think us glorious, I remind you of the way we forget

Lest you think us always cruel, may I point out to you the fact that we too have dreams

Lest the abysmal night calls our names and we answer, "Present"

I call unto the memories of the day to chase the dark seams

If fear our ignorance lingers
If doubt our certainty questions

I point to the hope which despite everything wonders
Blooms the rose in the most unpredictable of places

The butterfly that knows not that it is it that the roses admire

The bees who are oblivious to the nectar they produce
Humans to the poison into the earth they introduce

The shadows of me today meeting yesterday's faces

On How to Continue

Those who have good memories must reach out to their past to find gratitude for life as a reflection of their will to go on. Those with no past shall reach out to the future, those with neither shall dissect the present and find sparks of happiness in themselves, and if they are brave enough in the beauty of others' joy.

They must remember that the Moon, also coming from the depth of darkness, reflects a bright face looking towards the Earth.

Youth and Old Age

Four persons were sitting in the bus facing each other: on one side a boy and a girl under the age of five and on the other side two old men perhaps in their seventies. They all had the same look in their eyes; a look of frustrated expectations. Were they short-changed by life?

Mind Control

I was watching the news about a carnage that recently happened and a voice in me said, "Don't let evil entertain you." I turned off the TV, walked out of the house and the world was as brighter as it ever was and I understood.

On Life and Death

"Thank goodness that life is but a transition towards a transformation! Otherwise, we would have been bored of death." Said the hereafter.

You Said Ethnography?

What is the use of ethnography? For some, to justify yesterday's incredible lies through today's incredible bullshit.

On Nationalists

"They have a nostalgia for a world that never existed."

On Infatuation

"She took a part of me and never returned it back or was it I who imparted something to her without being asked to?" Love asks.

On the Fear of Death

Don't be afraid of death, it is a question of minutes if not seconds, but don't be sloppy about losing life for it endures longer in time.

On Free Will

Is it possible that free will is but a consequence of a frustrated dependence?

Haven't we observed that the more satisfied dependence is, the less freewill is called upon to exercise its royal functions?

The autonomous being, not a free one, as human beings are only rarely free, is perhaps that individual who understood through a repeated frustrated experience that is it in his or her best interest, better yet it is his or her responsibility, to take charge of one's own needs and to ferry them to shore on one's own terms.

The Body

There are those who perceive and treat their body as an enemy that they need to overcome or to subjugate. I see mine as a friend who has always carried me with great benevolence, and to whom I am grateful. I am not his slave as in friendship there is no slavery just as in that other noble order of things, I am speaking of love, there is no hate. When one day we go our separate ways, I would like him to know with gratitude that I loved him so much.

On Freedom

A human being cannot be free all the time, but being autonomous is a continuous possibility.

On Being Bad

"Am I a bad person?" Asked a man of a judge.
"No, you are a person who did bad things." The judge replied, "we have no choice, but to protect ourselves from you; you are a liability that needs to be neutralized "
"I see, and how are you planning to do that?
"The way the law sees it. In your case through the maximum of penalties. Luckily for you, we also need someone to put the fear of chaos in the

people, that is why, at some point we will let you loose."

Money vs. Fame

On the choice between fame and money, I choose money. Why continue to work if you do not have to? You will just be the most famous person in prison.

Strides

I row like the sun on the waves
My I accompany towards the decline

I see in the distance the past dying out

A child impassive in his destiny
I see him and he sees me, I contemplate him and he looks at me,

The child is I

We are a going and a coming

Towards the heavens a bird flies, it perches on the peaks of the Aether
Downward it drops a look of horror, does it see the future of our footsteps?

The wind in people's hearts picks up
Hate curbs the clear and distinct face of wisdom
Fear imprisons the will and in disdain takes the senses in divergence

In the distance, resolution of hope is in tatters

The eagle again looks down, always with the same horror he sees the weight of our existence

A weak sigh in eternity
An almost inaudible click under chains of strident sound

The eagle leaves his nest of clouds and regains the heights of the mountains
Below, the crowd disperses, remains an infant

Incomprehensible, yet with a common sense
Life, a rest out of the silence of the universe

He walks awkwardly, but not in vain

His future he sees as wants it the bee in itself

As promises it the sun with each sequence of its awakening

Beyond madness, he encounters the traits of wisdom in the becoming fate of the small seeds

He thinks he sees the eagle following him, his feet in the grass are lost under the weight of nature waking up

He makes strides of twenty years each

At twenty, he seeks himself amongst the hurricanes

At forty, he finds streaks of copper, a sun of yore

At sixty, he walks under the shade of the sun and waits

Happens whatever happens, he discharges his memories and seems to find his future of long ago

He measures his winters, he counts and understands

His horizon moves and rises

His stars for sure are much brighter

For sure life was never so benevolent;
He sees the galaxies nearer and space more welcoming

He wakes up early in the morning to meet up at the horizon with his benefactor because, he says, sleeping is good only for those who have less than twenty years and he is only a child

Impassive in his destiny

I see him and he sees me, I contemplate him and he looks at me, we see each other

On Posthumous Fame

Posthumous fame is like wreaths or bouquets of flowers offered to a beautiful woman now that she is a skeleton. They are there to give credit to the flowers or the giver of them rather than to the dead beauty.

A Thought

I am not dumb enough to believe that I am wise, I am not crazy enough to believe that I am a saint. I am not enough of a coward to pretend to be brave, neither am I less brave to let cowardice vanquish me. I am honest enough to see that at least in love I want more that the others.

On Books and Reality

Going through life, I realized how little writers know about life; they tend to project their imagination in time and space and it comes down infallibly short of the real world. Nothing awaits as is expected; it is either better or less, but never the same.

On Experts

There are those for whom showing annoyance continual criticism is a sign of being a great mind, whereas it is rather symptom of a great lack of self-confidence and of a voluntary blindness.

On Evil

Evil is something you do and is not something you are. You also are lucky if you can redeem yourself.

The Requiem

Though my body in stone of absentia is now encased
My soul, if you allow me, to the stars flies
Though much of me will fade under the weight of time

My presence of once is in eternity laced

I give thanks to the light that carried me so far
Never a friend of the shadows though I understand how we are

Like the birth of a ship expecting the sea
To tell its tale of oceans and the waves to be

My impact is as feeble as the tight grip of the fingers of a baby just born

To a heart torn between anticipation and a yearn

For love rightfully to earn

My sails fluttering their wings on liquid air
To find the maid that is imperfect, yet fair

To find a way where there is none

To heal the pain through the pouring soothing rain
All the way from the heavens and in between

Though the presence wished, memory is too subtle a scene

I see you from the present as I passed you unseen

Behind the veil of your eyes, beyond your mind's unflinching grip

I become what we are all meant to one day be

The course is set, the compass at the helm

A ghost vessel needs not to float
The truly happy needs not to gloat

True love needs not its object intentionally hurt
Though I observed that foolishness is not always a trait of the inert
Perfection needs no stifling art
Betrayal is a cowardly greed
Pride a common currency to heed

Though the choice is hard
Clarity for the willing is a valuable card

It is not a gamble, but a good and decent start

I am another you of the colour of the sky of the colours of the sea

I carry you like you carry me

The ocean melting into the sea

On Writing

At the heart of every writer lies a presumption, just like in every criminal, that he or she will not be caught in flagrante delicto and that the incriminating mistakes will not be revealed or seen by the prying eyes of the quizzing mind.

This is why one starts to write in delinquency and continues in maturity despite the evident flaws.

The Fool that is Us

"The difference between the wise and the fool is that the fool feels that he is, the wise knows who he is." I concluded once. Luckily there was no one to hear me, no one until I heard, "How do you feel?"

"I am a Homo sapiens among illustrious many, our lights from the Earth may one day be as brighter as yours." I responded to the inquisitive stars.

Having pity on me, one of the stars took me by the hands and I saw:

Vagrant waves tired of the sea

Stars crashing through space thirsty for a wish

Roses seeing obstacles in the bees

Butterflies chasing away the rainbow

On Being Inebriated

I don't need alcohol to see the world in its depths, I carry the sun in me.

What Sometimes Happen

They thought they ejected him, lo and behold, to their frustration, they saw him rise in propulsion.

Few Truths

A life worth living is not a life leased to someone else

A time well spent is a time fulfilled

Humans are not free, but autonomous when there is a will to be

On Responsibilities and Consequences

The poodle knows not to mess with the lion, and if it ever does, too bad for the poodle.

The Ugliest Show on Earth

Madness and misery are an ugly spectacle, but there's an ugliest one and it is self-delusion; it is the true enemy.

On Suicide

The reason people kill themselves is perhaps the same reason they have for being born; hubris. Ask yourself?

On Cockiness

Many misled souls misread conceited self-assertiveness for self-confidence and so they go about giving it a stock. Oblivious of how ridiculous they look, they go about proudly prancing like kings wearing but crowns of thorns.

On Bullies

I don't like bullies. The bully is a weak person trying to prove himself or herself by being aggressive and ending being beaten up; I reluctantly in self-defence do or approve of the beating.

On the Spontaneity of Love and Friendship

There's no such thing as a regimented friendship or love.

On Life

If life were a woman who shared the same feelings as me, I would have married her, but this not being the case, I actually had an equally good deal; life gave birth to me and treated me like a good mother her infant. I am always in amazement pampered.

Happy is the one who lives,
Happier is the one who knows it!

On the End of the Self

The entity that we are cannot on its own totally reject itself, and when it does, due to some external reasons, you get suicide.

To Someone I Accidently Met

"You look like someone dear to me and whom I miss so much; thank you for being!"

On Good Memories

I wish I were clever enough to remember these golden moments.

On Self-Advancement in Life

Without propulsion there is no projection, and it is, the propulsion, rarely external to the object it pushes up. Pressures come and go. To succeed you need to apply the same urge that keeps you from becoming extinct and, when you least expect it, life will give you a helping hand.

The Thing that is Life

Those who passed the same path are assured not to lose their way. You have been on this road, find your way. Find the urge and you will find the way. Loose it and you will assuredly end up in the crowded kingdom of regrets.

What We Must See

In the transparency of the day, he felt something intently looking at him, he looked up many times and saw nothing. Years later, not remembering that he ever did, he again felt the intent look, this time the sensations were vivid, but the source was still helplessly unseen, he looked up and saw it, an eye beaming down on him and his world.

On Standards

The strength of youth proclaims, "I affirm." Life softly responds, "I wait."

Nature produces an unbelievable beauty, Arrogance reduces it to a horrible state.

On Ownership

The clever owns, but is never possessed by what he owns.

On Self-restraint

Crying in public is like bleeding in public, they are both sad and equally messy.

On Movement and Thought

"I hope you gained a new perspective, now that you moved back and forth." Said the wall to the bird.

"I don't need to move to get perspectives, though it may help, I just need to fire up the right particles in my brain to be able to do so." The bird responded.

On Communism

It is as bellicose as capital. Wait, it is capital!

On Bad Politeness

Though, I agree with you this seat should go to whoever needs it the most, I care not for your rudeness towards me and the other passengers of the bus; it seems to me that you are one of those people who believe that they are allowed to be rough out of politeness.

On Anger

Whoever is able to anger you is able to control you.

On literary Posthumous Fame

The living does care about books, the dying and the dead not so much.

Some Rules

We have to admit the game was rigged
before we started to play

Prisoners of time and failed opportunities,
We pretend to have the choice to stay
We fail to see what is beneath our nose
Arrogance even next to the rose

We gather the little we seek
All that makes us less bleak

We falter, yet it is an easy trick
To keep anything, one must not be prompt to fade

To live forever one must not be of humanity or by humanity made

On Being Careful with What We Take In

Whatever echoes in, forced or allowed in, must echo out. One way or another a reflection or a deflection is made.

Altitudes

The shadows of tomorrow wave to the bystanders of today

The sunset lingers in the summits the sunrise used to call home

The peaceful invisible air rules supreme as its aurora makes way

The cool wind dries the tears before they fall
Time whispers or is it a call?
Life of itself flows imperceptible
Space unfulfilled clamours for sounds

Credulity of truth incredible; something is amiss, says the empty horizon with a hiss

Arrogance and judgement of themselves dope
Of the hanging, an empty rope

August covered by a haze
Eternity tempered by abrupt days
Evermore in a loving gaze

Who am I? Asks the breeze

Knows not humankind the appellation of the wind

Disappointment has no master or foe
No friend for the dying star ready to go

A barge awaits the diving soul
A window to the fleeting ground

A wave to the falling pulse

Here and there an incubation in time
Hatches the unknown universe

Indifference to the grind
Passivity in the heart of the mind

What goes up won't come down
Death, the resting place of dreams
What you own won't fetch a dime
What you trade is a ghost in the mine

The shadows off their seat they stand
The time to leave and arrive is outbound

From my memories I recollect roses in a beaming field
What wants must yield
Thus, of emptiness and fill
Thus, of ignorance and bliss

To love you must know how to give
To care you mustn't just receive

To be forgiven you must repent
To repent you mustn't break that which you have bent

Your memory of its misgivings must be as sharp as is attentive vagueness of its amnesic proceedings

What I have known carries on in time
Leaving the whisper of the ghost to find an unlikely thought

An infant of eternity unbound

Of judgement I point to the burning tar
A mask of what is hidden inside

A flame insatiable to burn itself and the world around

Who knows best knows less
Who knows little shouldn't proclaim to know what causes a mess

If you hold a grievance remember that it can pass
From one to the other is short fence

Ingratitude is heavier than sudden
If you carry, you have a burden

If you linger, you somewhat surpass

If you think you rule, take a short trip in time
A soldier to the hungry Mars, splinters of seconds to the age
Hope to the blinding rage
You are but fodder to your entourage

Time does not tick, it flows like Aether unbound
It sails like the stars unfathomable
You don't reach for them, they come to you in waves of light
Remarkable is their surge
Perception is a matter of urge

Confidence without arrogance is the attraction
The balance is acting in absentia
Finding the way takes movement and no inertia

If you see you don't perceive
If you look you are bound not to…

On Courage

Ignorance also gives courage.

On Our Species

If you feed wolves and humans to keep their ravages from the children then go ahead, but don't expect any gratitude from the herds of beings, but of the wolves you may perhaps find some.

On Self Discovery

"How would a kid know the bounds of its force and personae without testing the springs of gravity?

How would the eagle learn to soar if it is kept within the webs of the infringing cage?

How would pain recede if it is not followed by the relentless waves of relief?

Surely the fire that lit the night was but a combustion that burned"
"Bear with me please." Says life as it gives life to the Universe

On Things that Matter

That which matters when you are dying is what matters most if you make it through.

Primeval

A bird flies through the depth of the clouds, he swerves past the falcons and the eagles soaring high, he lands on the surface of the day on a place called Fawn

He pulls an arrow from his side, the wound could have been mortal, he recalls the distances and places he saw

He says, "Time is ripe for the willing." With his beak he points to the dawn

Across the river, crocodiles swim upstream hiding in the water washing steam

By the foot of a hill, ants, busy building a fortress to stand against time, move in a circuitry of awe

Across the bay, past the river, the mountains courting the sky, he still sees the glitter of the sea

An imprint in his mind's eyes is the vision

Dolphins racing the waves making time
Their course is to become, to dive deep, make arcs in the air, lullaby the earth, paint the sky

A young tiger, well fed, his paws folded, in a zoo cage, contemplates the horizon, places he could have been

He sniffs at the free ants, his breath in particles breaks away through the prison bars, but him not

He wishes he could likewise rise up into the heavens to meet the stars

He knew them to be there behind the scene

If he could only tell them his story, assuredly they would sympathize

Freedom is too precious to be pawned
Time is too short to be wasted in a bottomless pit of regressions

In the distance he sees the bird, falcon and eagles

Though far away, he senses the crocodiles on the river ruling the bay

Time seems to halt and obey
In his eternity, he ponders the day

On Banks

A bank is but honesty with a premium. At least this is what it is supposed to be.

On Sunset

At sunset you see a mix of humanity's regrets and some wishes coming true, thus the exploding and contrasting colours.

On Our Behaviour

In ourselves we carry echoes of every good or stupid ideas imparted in us, each in turn bouncing against each other and against us. The important thing is to recognize them for what they are and flush out the stupid ones into the abyss of insignificance where they belong; we are all capable of acting stupid, but the question is are we willing to continue to do so?

On Learning and Books

A book of lessons is as good as the will of the person willing to learn from it.

On the Divine Plan

The fact that things never end well for the rest of the creatures in this world does not seem to bother the least those who think that there is a divine plan.

On What You May Hold True

Thousands of years of structured lies.

To the Belligerent

You are like an animal in a cage. Pumped up with anger and nowhere to go. You are making a spectacle of yourself. I, on the hand, am free, caged animals are a rarity to me. You are an interesting phenomenon, Kinda like a bug.

On the Need of Enlightenment

We literally go half asleep through life.

The Solace in Space

Shall we to the Gods for the obvious find a prayer?
Shall we beg of the certain odds a soothsayer?

But to temper our doom
To postpone our gloom

Rain drops fading under the disproportionate heat of the desert sun

"If I don't kill you, I will burn you in hell!" The purported fates chant

At every unreasonable turn the sun is bent

In the spider's web, the ant is ordered to find deliverance

In the deluge to build its fortress

Of order a semblance
Chaos in the heart of the balance

No right is given but in time billed with remonstrance

The ant's luck is to recognize its end
Find the best in the circling sand becoming mud

Yet, the ant doesn't beg and despite the odds builds a dome
Despite the recurring rain makes a home

With the thorns it makes a way to its morn
Beyond the germs and diseases, it distils health

The ant learns to fly without wings
To measure her life through time
To record their story under the stars

To talk and see through the veil of space

To light her world like the moon's face

To build his mountains so to scrape the sky

The ant paints with words and is aware,

"I see my end as vapours in the sand
Mine are the things that mend

The Earth its seeds to the universe outbound
Life making a sound

If you don't believe me watch the ground"

On Holy Books

When you concede to a so-called divine book, you concede your brain to it, and to the manner in which it is interpreted by anyone else. You become a willing hostage to its inclinations and rearranged patterns. In brief, you lose control.

On Nationalism

As rigid and regimented as religion. Wait, it is a religion!

On What We Truly Are

Many of us have two faces, after all we keep all that is unpleasant in us away from the people we love, and many of us are like the moon whose dark side is kept hidden and when it is revealed we realize that it is not much different from what we have known it to be; we kept hidden that which we all knew all along to be there.

On Eternity

Futility, the aspiration of the neon flashing light

Eternity, the sure path of every demise for in the state of non-existence everything is eternal

Far Away

Take the moon and, aye, the sunshine
The soft rain and the birthing of the rainbow
A clear blue sky

The fear of death and the promises of life
The cool breeze, the peaceful evening, the relief
at the end of the unforgiving strife

Now you may have a shot

A homeless finding a welcoming shelter away from the frost of December

A bird finally reaching shore, leaving behind the angry oceans

Yes, you may have a shot

Take the four seasons, mix them in a cup
Drink them in one shot and you may see what I am looking at

Mystical like the fall
Colours borrowed from heaven
Foliage stolen from the garments of the gods,
From way back when the angels said out loud our names instead of a shudder, a whisper

Sinking not in an ocean, not a river, but in the haze of June, calling out your name in the darkest of nights

Not a prayer, but best wishes for you to linger a rising star
Have you ever missed that which is there?

Clueless is the shadow to its maker

Does the horizon see its creation?
Fading away particles seeking an earthly home
Neither is true beauty of the reason for the enthralled gazer

On Good Readings

An inspiration fee, paid in equal fashion, is what we owe to great thinkers.

On Becoming

"We can't all be strong!" Exclaimed the voice of uniformity.
"I am not asking you to be strong, I am asking you not to be weak." Quietly answered the voice of individuality.

Nature's Tablet

"Thou shalt live in clarity." Orders the sun.
"Thou shalt seek balance." Says the mid-day.
"Thou shalt dream." Paints the sunset on the horizon.
"Though shalt find a purpose for your soul." Says the spirit.
"Thou shalt find but me when all else is gone." Cautions the soul.
"Thou shalt find a bed for your weary body and a roaming world for your spirit." Says the night.

"Thou shalt wake up." Commands the sunrise.

If We Could See

Tiny squirrel, you risk your life under the tires of the machine for nuts that do freely fall from the sky

People, through hate you become cellmates of prisons whose doors where never meant to be yours to pry

Worker, you toil as if there is always a tomorrow
They accuse you of every imaginable thing, but never of giving up, though as you can see you never reach your arrow

Trader, you count your gains, you spread your riches like the heavens do the stars
Yet, you hardly see your child smiling at you while you count the time you convert in solitary golden bars

Soldier, you celebrate wars, you carry a glaive,

You fly killing machines made of bauxite and steel
You do not see the sun rising and the birds flying towards freedom in one leap

Your enemies are also brothers in combats by war made destitute

Just like you, their parents, children, friends, and loved ones in torment are praying for a peaceful substitute

Necktie wearing fox, you think you're shrewd and hide behind the soldier and his fence

The forest conceals you just like the crowd its grins and the pretentious minds their ignorance

You do not seem to know your past

Yet, you meet it without being alert

Just as the sand in its greed unwillingly the desert it asserts

You laugh to the sound of the cruising mast

Your realm is the red of the slaughter

The edges of the cliffs and the turpitude of all that cannot be honesty washed with water

In you I do not see myself

King maker, I believe I have seen traces of you on the sand

You are as invisible as silence, yet on approaching the palpable we see your steps,
The darkness and the sun are to you incurable,
Your eye looks at me, yet you have more one too many sets,
You are incomprehensible to me, a lot of potential, yet…

Heart of hay that is mine, I used to believe that you were honest, brave and of improvement
Now to me your insignificance is of your movement

Your palpitations are an electric charge that you toss in the air
Not knowing what is good nor what is fair

The harbour of your chills reminds me of the thick layer of painting the artist leaves behind his braided masterpiece
An effort, an attempt, but not a centrepiece

I am the judge, you are torment
I am going away, leaving you unbent

Chance wants it and so does my intent

The fatality of madness is a risk of longitude
The wind carries the noise of our still solitude

The key to our existence, we reduce to a "why"
Living seems simply too narrow to try

So, we languish watching out for death which never was a choice

Happy is he who understands before to this world he adds his voice

On Freedom

The knowledge of his or her state of serfdom never set a slave free, though a good start it is. It is actually finding the way to be free is what does it.

On Fame and Shame

The price of fame is shame and the price of infamy is fame. Both are not necessarily deserved.

On Actions

"*The wise man regards the reason for all his actions, but not the results.*" - Seneca.

I could not resist by updating it to:

"A wise man regards the reason for all his actions FIRST, but a wiser man may do likewise and also MIND the results to remedy their consequences."

Some Truths

Deceitful are my principles if I do not want to save a child

Woe on us as our children share our flaws, but fortunately for the world they are not doomed to inherit them

Despite the pretentious attempts of the clouds the sun does not cease to shine

If the night glows, it does it only through the aid of the stars

And if the rivers descend from the heights of the mountains as do the goats ascend the elevations, the summits are nonetheless prohibited even to the impetuous seas

Yet, the gentle sparrows in air find gravity easy to climb and make of their peaks joyful racing courses

And though money is convertible into countless goods, yet, goodness remains a precious recourse when truth corners us in isolated turns

Despite the fact that time keeps an eye on us and that we end up losing sight of it during its frantic race

And if the sun in perpetuity us leaves, we know that at least for those we love it will tomorrow continue to shine

It is just that our star has found a new course

It leaves us after it allowed us to glow as bright as it shines

And if tomorrow our shadow does not palpitate,

In a repose of solitude, we leave it for it is its turn to unriddle us in eternity

If our soul laughs in our face as it sees itself of the extent of space and us but another course

We have the memory of the flow of its personality in delirium as one too many,
Its gaze allows us to see in the depths of our body the weakness of the traveller without roots,
As sees the anchored tree the sand by the wind being dispersed

Our shared tears are made by the dried-up sun into vitreous vapour

Clinging to the harbour of our turpitude, we contemplate the truth of our reflection

In the mirror of time, weariness looks out for the spurts of our lack of attention

Truth finds only those who want to cease it in the air like the rays do at the bedside of the sun at the gates of the horizon,
In an evening of peace in need of an aberration

Splendid as a life rich in gratitude at the end of the horizon

And if the angels drop down on earth, we must recognize them in the smiles of children
With an almost adult look observant as the eyes of the gods in solitude on earth

In the sound of the dolphins chanting the sea

In the colours of the shooting stars joining time in its race against eternity

In the sound of the dead passing on in infinity

I see but particles drowning in doubt

In the finality of indecision

A tree in bloom with leaves as white as severity
A weight as heavy as helplessness
A lightness of heart as that of the spirits

Yet, I fly as do the birds in the wind of hope

On Reality

What to you is logically real, may be factual alright, but it may not be as real as you may think. Example: let us assume, at face value, that the number of books an author sells is representative of the wide appeal of a certain genre in a given time. Seeing the rise of sales of a particular book, one may logically assume an equal rise of interest in our society in its subject matter, and, if the subject in question was not a popular line of interest, one starts to assume a certain shift in society's behaviour. What if, I, being a rich and eccentric person not knowing what to do with my money, decide to spend millions purchasing copies of a book whose absurd subject is "How to save the dodo?" I know they are long extinct so please humour me. I do the purchasing of the book via many of my businesses and affiliates and distribute these books through different channels so that at the end of the tally no one knows who actually bought them and as far as the general public is concerned the book is a hit due to its spectacular sales.

This being done, you start to assume a real rise in society's sudden interest in helping the dodo survive, taking this variable as part of a reality check, you correctly pronounce judgment on how dump people are, and though your logic is sound, I managed to manipulate it towards my eccentric ends.

Now imagine what people with hidden agendas and unlimited resources can do?

Nature from a distance

I love nature and have respect for it, but I will not put a stick where the bears sleep.

On the Devil

The first trick the Devil performed on humanity was to create religion. The second one was to coerce/convince decent people to surrender to it, but his ultimate and masterful act was to convince them that he actually exists.

On Laws and Morals

I suspect that many people do not commit crimes, not because religion told them not to or because of their inklings for justice, but because they have an innate interest in preserving their assets. Thus, they are doomed in passing laws and taking any measures, many times at the expense of those weaker than them, in preserving them; this being their condition in time and space, you will find that every group since the dawn of history has done the same.

The necessity being established as the source, one needs to focus on the merits of these laws and whether or not their punishments are proportional to the infractions committed.

On Being Hyped Up

Tears are a very expensive commodity; don't waste them on insignificance.

On Dreams and the Absurd

The themes of a given dream are sometimes but the interpretation of the changing ambient temperature of the body, due to external changes of temperature in the environment, by consciousness in its state of temporary erasure named sleep. Sometimes, we find that when it is cold, we dream of rain and if we are too hot or feverish, we end up having nightmares. On the other hand, if we are really comfortable, we dream of a state of gentleness.

Occasionally, in the wakefulness state of being and its dimension, we indulge in this state of dream voluntarily and lucidly; we call this hope.

When it is time to be resurrected, consciousness throws an absurdity our way and we wake up.

On Literature

Literature, in sum, tries to give us the experiences of life without its sequelae or its exorbitant consequences as observed or personally paid for by the author.

Thus, when it is a successful, Literature is a laboratory of the real world.

On Bad Luck

Bad luck is always in search of followers and it finds them mostly amongst the pessimists.

Questions

What happens to our world when we are asleep?

What happens to our selflessness when we grieve?
Where is our charity when under the weight of anger off benevolence we secede?
Where is our goodwill when overindulgent in courage and fear we forget to breathe?

On Infatuation and Love

Infatuation is the spark, it is necessary for the birth of love, just make sure it doesn't burn homes.

On Men Without Women

Men, at first glance, are like the colourful productive pollinating bees, but without the flowers, women, they are an annoying senseless noise catering to an overindulged queen; their ever-inflated ego.

On Nature's Plan

There's no plan in nature, it is all profusion of life. What we call rules are observations bound to happen and are of the realm of humanity in its way to surpass its nature.

Innocence and the End of the World

The end of world is coming, these people say. So, the world was after all not well thought through from the start; I am just a child, I was born yesterday and they are now telling that God is going to end it soon.

On Chance and Results

Good luck does oddly favour the relentless and those who continue and persevere in their search for the answers.

On Who You Are

Your self is not something you are, it is something you continually build. So, instead of saying "I am", you have to think "I am being".

On Justice

The concept of justice is not in nature, I am not saying this to be mean nor to blame, but to note a fact. A fact which should hold some weight in your thinking.

On Nature

She is not perfect, so don't resent her, but she is prolific; she produces in profusion.

On Truth

The truths of the past are easy to accept, but those of the present are much harder and sometimes never admitted. We observe death, we live, we die, and we move on to other things.

The end is evident and yet we resist to the end. Is it me or is there a line of thought here?

The Genesis of Life

Life dared the silence of the world and to punish it death was born.

On Trusting Your Heart

"Trust your heart." Some say.
I ask, "do we spend fortunes to send our kids to expensive educational institutions to listen to their hearts? Is it not so that they can learn to

reason better?" If this is not the case, then we should leave them home and dispense with the resources somewhere else.

Trust only reason, and your intuition, if to the test, it proves to be reasonable.

On Life

We know the dream to be absurd, all we need to do is to find the element causing its absurdity.

Life and its Condition

To perpetuate itself, life is in need of conditions, we must not confuse them with rules or laws as when we say "the laws of nature" for these are mere inventions of humanity and are non-existent in nature, and these conditions are amoral; nature does not bear judgment, but humans do.

This explains the contradictions of nature as it is conditional and unreasonable.

The more civilized a human being is, the more he or she sees the world through a moral optic, and the more a person is in nature the more he or she carries with him or her the germs of the unexpected of natural life. Cruelty being in the state of nature, he or she carries it with him or her and is always pivoted against it due to his or her condition of civility.

All existence or nonexistence has a condition and if we know the condition, we do not equally know the reason, if there is any, but we can always observe its condition which is the same; existence or nonexistence.

The reason or reasons are of argumentative and circular nature.

On Death

Death is the dissemination of what we are into what we will become.

On Taking Control of Your Future

Don't let a bad tricks plaid on you become a wicked spell. Convert misdirected passes into great scores.

On Long Expected Gifts

Sometimes, long awaited power is suddenly given to you, and in your excitement, you accept it without asking any questions. Why would you? Wasn't' this long due? Yet, as you will learn, this was done only to give you an opportunity to hang yourself by letting you tie the noose.

Endurance

I am the rock that the sea in its fury attempts to rampage only to see it come out polished

I am the foundation of all that is solid and yet bearably light; I am a spark becoming light

I am fluidity today, hardened tomorrow, no I am not a volcano, I am a thought becoming reality

A Regret

The time that is running away, I would have caught it
The harbour that recedes, I would have held it
Seasickness, I would have healed it

The probe seeking depth, I would have shown it to the summits of my intentions
I would have given it memories, the impassable rocks of the future to sustain

Puffs of promises, the wisps of light and darkness of the horizon to embellish

The desperate stubbornness of the bison facing the moving ocean which moves in order not to move

Life, a miracle despite everything
Raison, a pure season

To swim in the air by flying over the clouds; to bathe in the Aether
To madly find one's happiness as one's steps are found in the oceanic night
To feel the rocks and on tiptoes extend oneself to touch the stars

To hear the wind partake in your awakening and carry the life-giving scent of your breath
Despite the igneous flame that burns the water in the deep so it can burst out in fire and earth
Despite the weight of the heart, which like an anchor treads over the surfaces and meets its gravity in the depths of the oceans

Lost is the dolphin in pursuit of the seductive looks of the stars as in the heavens they set sail

Flies consciousness to the rescue of sleep
Passes the bee on the vastness of petals

The Earth curves at the spell of the horizon

The horizon, under the lure of the stars, folds under the weight of the memory of the fleeting season

The race which time loses and empty space gains

A maxim that the wind chants, and life sweeps aside

A lesson that we learn only once ahead of the body and soul, and looking back we see them marching in solitude

Yet, despite everything we charge towards the passing future

The memory and the night

The ocean, the embers, and the sound of the wind that rhymes

A life that propagates

The stop sign screaming, "beware of memories!",

The rain that tells us of what is in the depth of the soul that astounds,

The earth that trembles, I would have soothed it
The closing in harbour, I would have warned it
The sea that is leaving, I would have searched for it

The Mirror

There are many bad fates, one of the worst ones ought to be being reincarnated as a mirror; living a lifetime without having a personality, denude as it is of character, is a thought which ought to bring the most soulful spirits down.

Yet, many are…

On Pride and Country

Shall we be tied up to a spot, a place, a country, a planet, a solar system, a galaxy just because we happen to be born there by happenstance? Shall we continue to stupidly take pride in what

is but a natural coincidence? Shall we allow ourselves to continue to be defined by it?
I say no, hell no!
Thus, I part myself with this question.

One More Positive Thing in the World

In a few hours there will be a sunrise, we may not be there to see it, but that is, the sunrise, a good thing in itself.

What We Must Relearn

There are no dumber than those who believe to know.

There are no more arrogant than those who believe themselves to be humble.

Thus, I subtly make my confession.

On Learning

The hardest lessons are the ones that from ourselves we do not learn.
The everlasting ones are those we are not able to forget.

The Summits and the Lowlands

Is this the order of our redemption? To see what is to be before what is?

To find before we intent to search
To leave as the curtains still hang

To puzzle at the obvious and sift not that which is begging for our eyes to see

Never cared for glory and golden chains,
But to see your face I dared with them to acquaint for a while

To contemplate the vain grazing on the low lands

to see the sane called to the stand and the fools giving the keys of the land

Meaneth time to suffer our indulgence and soften our resolve?

To witness our persistence and laugh at our approaching silence?

Dare not the summits challenge the sky?
The lover, the flames of his heart with tears to absolve?

The firefly, the night?

Could it be that silence is but a distraction from the noise of the mind? From that voice, which ceases not to ponder and echoes as strangers of each other do wonder?

Your voice neath the shadows of silence my will to carry

To the Sun piercing the horizon

To the ocean soothing the crying rain

To the days that last forever and the memories chiselled in the heart that say so

Could it be that an instance of itself seeks semblance like echoes do the sound?

Like an eye seeking a gaze?

Like darkness in the abyss awaiting the light

Extenuating circumstances expecting relief

The mountain, in the mist seeking a companion?

Sharpness, an edge?

And Eternity, life?

Kindness, a friend?

Who said that to live one must and to die one shouldn't?

Our way is the sunset, but our end is the stars where we will return

To those who seek kindness and not a price,
My equals through the horizon of time and space,
To them a short distance in salutations

The Aether to the stars

My presence in this moment as is yours to find

A touch of semblance through the cracks of time

On Heaven and Hell

Heaven and Hell are two mirrors and it depends on who is looking at them. That is why most of us like the first mirror and few of us dare to or survive the trip looking into the second one and always see someone else in it.

On Life

Life; that brittle thing in the barren eternity lasting for billions of years.

On Nations

Nations? Pride in being part of the crowd! That is indeed a slap on the face of priceless intellect.

Shrinks Analysed

It takes a special person to become a shrink, to go about analysing everyone else except oneself; are you not running away from your own problems as you embrace those of the others? Does the void of the multitude offer you an open vault to the self so that you do not have to lift the lid of your own? I wonder what is it that is lurking underneath, waiting for the patients to leave so it can come out and play?

Trust

"I trust you, but I do not trust your judgment" – *On not being blind to the mistakes of people we love*

Power to the People

We are told by some that the people are manipulated and intoxicated by propaganda and this is why they cannot tell the truth from the lies that are predominant in our current political system; we need to get rid of the corrupt elements and return power back to the people, namely, to the people who were so easily duped and on whom we will have to entrust our future security.

Either the first argument is wrong or the solution does not make any sense. Could they be both?

The Flagrant Flaw of the Good

Crusaders always neglect those who matter most; their loved ones.

On the Right to Question Everything

How can I have a critical mind if I don't dare question everything? If I question myself, what makes you and your truth any holier?

On Sensitive Minds

Tombs with wreaths on them are but indication of recent and fresh wounds.

The Weakness of Evil

Fire needs to burn itself in order to burn anything else, it must carry injury in its core before it gives it to the rest of the world, there lies it weakness.

On Not Being Challenged Enough

A static conformist mind is hardly a creative mind, now a radiating mind, that is something worth gazing into for this is where great ideas leap from.

Science's Religious Skeletons

I find it very troublesome that the bright mind that came up with the theory of how the universe came about, but reflected a long-held belief that order comes out of chaos. I also find it convenient that everything theorized after that but follows the same geometrical patterns.
- *On the Big Bang Theory*

On History

Read the history of the people, take any country, and you will find the disgusting slobbering of its politicians all over it.

The Dream that Will Never Be Satisfied

To be the other and remain oneself.

On Murder

A time will come when with abhorrence future generations will look at the fact that we eat animals, but with less chagrin they will regard our killing of each other for they will still be doing it themselves.

Learning Sources

Out of the distance of the stars from each other,
I find that space is a matter of perception

Out of the flow of water, its persistence in carving veins on the surface and the deep, that assertive patience endures there where vehement rash fades with no trace

Out of the generosity of the sun, glorious in its rise and fall, that you must have that which you want to give and be of equal grace when you leave

From the invisible wind in its might, manufacturing hurricanes out of imperceptible thin air, that power is not given, it is something you shape out of bare elements

From the memory of the wound as it gives birth to a scar, that the pain recedes, but that its links to the past remain

Out of the locked doors cautiously shut, that trust is not freely granted and that you must not necessarily need a key to enter

Out of the limitless expanse of the horizon, not to be narrow minded, the extent of your vision is what makes the world you know today and tomorrow

Your perception you need to control for if you don't someone else surely will

From the unfathomable will of the people that generalizations and statistics are but vain attempts to uniform nature

Un ugly intent to veil colours

From myself, I learned that I am full of it, and I leave it at that.

On Honesty

Nothing like a reaffirmed purpose to keep us honest; the premises are best when they go well with the conclusion.

A Consolation

Aye, the shadows are mighty and the weight is as real as is the surge

The end is palpable and the hope dumbfounded Yet, through the clouds a hand is extended; a comfort in the tears of a friend and those who give damn

There is satisfaction in the eyes of an adversary coming to make sure we are indeed dead and not knowing that through hate one is already embalmed; for there's no worse enemy of consequence than a satisfied vengeful urge

Aye, the sinking of the ship leaves the heart in distress afloat, yet, the unsinkable knowledge of the lit candles renders death but a chore

The frost, a gate to of the eternal night, may be frigid, but the warmth of a contented life is a tropical paradise in which the ice will melt and the thoughts will endure

As we become what we were always meant to be; a thought

We gaze at the world with the apprehension of the shooting stars and the glory of the sun as it unveils the day

We converse with the waves of our soul as it flutters its wings before it sails to the moon now covered by misty clouds

Aye, the night is of the unknown and so is the mystery from where we birth

Yet, the vibrations of the universe still in us unfold

The promise, even if for a short while, is fulfilled

The light that was once bright still in the darkness shows the way

The fear that once was mighty is now but an observation
That which was is no longer in evidence strange

That which "is" can no longer interfere
A mind in itself appears

Fade the illusions of grandeur
Sets the sun of illustrious wretchedness
The pomp of sedating madness

Grateful, always for the sunrise lighting the soul

Awakening, the dormant particles to reality the of the whole

The light notes of a tune, long forgotten, re-emerge

Obliterated is grief

That which is

Few Observations

King is not, he who is not king of his time
Rich is not, he who lives on borrowed time
Poor is he who of himself is a zealot

On Impressions

We barely know ourselves, less the others; what we call knowledge, of ourselves or others, is more often than not but impressions we have of each other. These impressions are dictated by the environment, where most of us spend our time, and those who spend most of time at work are just living their impressions as dictated by this particular environment. Likewise, their colleagues, also in the same vein, judge them on this impression and feel better about themselves through the belief that they know them and are warranted in their adopted impressions. Down deep, though, we all know that as the roles change so do the impressions, yet we stubbornly cling to a single one as being truer than the others.

Yet, few are true to the impression we have of them and when they do, society tends to hold it against them.

On Being Surprised of Disappointment

No one can get into your heart if you don't let them in first. There should not be a surprise on how they got in there.

The Seed in the Tree

What is the percentage of the seed in the tree? What is the percentage of the tree in the grown seed? How can we tell the seed from the grown tree or vice versa?

If you have paused, I ask, what is the percentage of a child in the man or woman? What is it that unites them through time and space? Is it perhaps their individual memory or perhaps their common one? Is there another unit that does last beyond consciousness? What is that thing that you may take away, and which if it is no longer present, cancels all of them and makes their self-awareness fade away?

Because we know that humanity is fixed in time and it is continuously being, we can presume that the thing that continuously change, the constant of change, is what we are after; it is the link between the seed and the change, and it is obvious that once a creature stops altering it ceases to exist.

Slow death is then the low reduction of the rate of change, quick death is the accelerated rate of change followed by an all system halt; uninterrupted change in between is life.

The above state is observed by humanity looking at itself, but is that the case in nature where everything is a constant transformation?

To nature, humanity, as a matter like any other, is eternal for it moulds it from one shape to another, and in that particular pattern humans are shapeshifters but never the same.

The above being said, I realize that I digress, sorry, I just saw a butterfly. Yes, we started looking for the element of that which is and is constantly being.

It seems to me arduous to seek the being in order to find the what is. Equally challenging is to find the present without the past.

Let us look at memory and note that it is no more enduring than the rest of components of the human body. There are people who lost their memory, yet their self, though tattered, is still functional; it still has a sense of the what is, some sense of the what was, and the constant of the being. So, memory is important, but it is definitely not the unit that we referred to earlier and during sleep it is turned off.

Common memory does not hold water either, it cannot sometimes even tell that the past is written as we speak and is never in agreement with other individual memories in recording events. Yes, it functions as a certain reference point, but, as the wise have long realized, it is easy to temper with, and is tempered with by the powers that be, and is therefore unreliable. It also is, during sleep, turned off.

Consciousness can be turned off, such is during a total anaesthesia, which element is in charge then? Though there is, it is definitely not Consciousness.

Is it that unit that turns them on and off? So, what is it? The one thing that in semblance seems to allow others to do the same for it? The thing, which during sleep is still on, and when memory is fading still keeps some order in place? The thing that is present in the crazy who still knows that money buys food, and in the sane who sells priceless time for it? The one thing running the animal and the human alike?

When all is stripped of its evolutionary skin what is it that is left to us to hold in our hands? A seed or a butterfly? If none of them then what is it?

On Religion as the Source of Morals

Religion has as much to do with morals as funeral halls with weddings. Namely, nothing.

On Cruelty

It is not about whether one is cruel or not, humankind is cruel, we are part of nature and look at what we have done to it, it is about whether one is to cease to be as such and what is one going to do about it.

On the Worst in People

One hears, "boy, for sure this one knows how to bring out the worst in people!"
I ask, "Is it possible that the worst was trying to come out anyway?"

The Wise and the Fool

"What did the fool say to the wise man?"
"Who are you?"
"What does the wise man say to himself?
"I am a fool. What will I do to cease being one?"

A Trick of the Trade

The "I", perceiving its end, tricks the body into submission, through the promise of an afterlife, so that it can continue its journey into the night.

The Soul in Poetry

In the matter of the spirit vs the soul, whether they exist or not is of no relevance to the poet, the spirit fades, but the soul rises.

On Threats as Arguments

The language of death is not a language of persuasion.

On Certitude

The arrogance of a certitude is as harmful as an intrepid ignorance.

On Beauty

"You are beautiful!" He said.
"Oh, thank you!" she replied.
"It is not a complement" He continued.
She looked puzzled.
"I made you think." He blinked and walked away.

On Some Misconceptions

Some of the rich think that all of us want to be like them, they don't seem to grasp the fact that many of us don't care about their life style, and many of us do not give a damn about their possessions, most importantly they think that their lives are so fantastic that we must want to be them. The truth is that, if asked, most of us want to be free of the financial burden and not necessarily be rich.

Some of poor think that self-righteousness was bestowed upon them only and that there are few rich that have it. They don't have the vision to see that being rich is just a life style, a comfortable one, they are right to assume, but which does not free one from the unavoidable incidents of life.

What You Make of it

A sad song won't make your lonely unless you are already there

The brevity of time won't make you brave unless you have an ounce of it in the depths of your inner breath

Love is not something you borrow, it is not for sure something you pay, ask a mother of her child?

Mirrors don't make people look good, it is their illusion that says their sharpness is mild

Money may buy things back, but it won't bring back the uniqueness of time,
The day that passes is as single as its end

What you fix you may not mend, ask the mother of her child

From the lies we know the truth is not born
It wraps itself sometimes with a thorn

No sunrise is aware of the dawn
No goodness of its malevolence
No evil of the evidence of its demise

And so, you and I and what we are, one in all, one in one or none at all

A happy song won't make your winter a sunny season

Neither will expensive clothing, your faltering heart a rallying cry

No unearthed shiny matter will buy you a soothing lullaby

Look at a parent burying a child

No divine order can explain or define

Watch the hypocrisy in the revolutions of the straight line

Mind your perspective in confinement defined

Hope is free, disappointment, though pricey, is not a crime

On Religion and Free Will

A god that created me free and autonomous, yet, tells me how and what I should think.

The Benevolent Star

I greet you in the morning free of charge, my sentences are balanced like the aura of my rays

Like to the sentient wisdom of self-retinue bay

I will tell you stories if you want to listen
Beauties under my shadows glisten

Hungry eyes seeking words to say

Curving rivers, landing lanes that shine like melted steel

Heart of stone vaporized by love's subtle build

Doors shut, now open by the streaming lightness of sound

Silence speaking her name, you knew she was there before you held the passing torch of fame

The earth is stable, yet you feel the shaking ground

The approach is imminent, you grow wings with every echoing of her curvature

Time is heavy or it does not exist, you cannot just find the aperture

You move through solid matter

The world is crowded, though in your loneliness the only face you see is hers

Eternity seems closer as you breathe her presence

The distance expands as the steps make way

You hear a recurring theme, but you know for certain that this is everything but a dream

The shadows' awkward brightness light the scene

You suspect treachery, but they are cleverer than that, they leave it to your clarity to help you fade

In the distant future you understand the efforts of the waves

The platitude of the knaves

The fate of every wreck

My light I give it, but you still have to leave your cave

My warmth is comfort, but you must know how to abide by the gravitational rules

I am here ever and ever, and like you I too must fade

You know me to be there for I keep my promise

Adhere to my code to find a respectful abode

I deliver no cheap reverence; my inclinations are equally curved

That which is owned by the many is owned by no one

No nation can claim me for the universe is my home

I rise every time you decide to see me; just close your eyes in you is that spark of delight

If you have not found it, my hint to you is that which, when you close your eyes, is trying to see through

The night is supreme, I grant, but it would be nothing without the light of the stars

On the Power of Nuisance

Importuned by a bee, a person does not see the splendour of the sun.

Religion and Blasphemy

All religions are a blasphemy against God, and since there none, they are instead but aberrations to humanity.
Luckily for their followers, it has to be said, that there is no such a vindictive entity for whereas the atheist says there is no God, religion goes further and makes a caricature of him.

Religions attempt to justify the Creator and interpret for the foreseeable future his last words, they claim to holders of his last messages, yet, they preach the opposite of what is professed in the way he created the world.

They all call for the veiling of that which the Almighty clearly created naked; why don't we put pants and dresses on dogs and cats and call it part of the divine revelation? Religion then professes to know better than what is revealed by the Creator to everyone to see through his creation.

If God wanted his created humans, dogs, cats, lions, bears, et. al. to wear pants, burkas or any other veiling assortment, he would have created them wearing them; does man believe he knows better?

Yes, lest I be misquoted, we need clothes, out of a human sense of decency, but most importantly if we want to survive in the hostile and lethal environment in which we are told a Creator in his wisdom puts us in and if the evidently godless competition of nature, animals consuming plants and being consumed by other animals, does not kills us, then bacteria and viruses will make sure to do the job.

Religions invented holy wars and capital punishment as they knew down deep that killing is also another blasphemy against the Creator; to kill means to know better than the divinity that created the person whose life is ended by the faithful, it is an evident attempt to terminate what is deemed to be a harmful creation; a mistake from the part of the Creator.

Thus, God creates, and again religion knowing best, kills.

No sane person who knows God can kill for murder is by principle an atheist act. It intends to says, if you are a theist, "I know that god made this person, but I know better, I will kill him or her, why not both? so that there is order where there was none before."

Religions being mostly male dominated, since the dawn of time, are chiefly preoccupied with ordering women; a cast-based system with man, no pun intended, always on top of the echelon.

This is why God is ever referred to as "He", even though most of them agree that the divinity, if it is unique, can never be but genderless. Try to pass it as a "She" in a place of worship and you will see the fury of disapproval hurled at you; you may get away with it if you are a man, they forgive your ignorance, but forget it if you are woman as they will consider this a challenge to their authority.

This brings me to the point of genderless beings or asexual beings; since the Maker of the universe is genderless, how come this never was the inspiration of religions? Why aren't they inspired to be like their maker? Why don't we see their leaders by droves voluntarily castrating themselves, ouch, and calling unto their members to do the same? Of course not, for sex is very important to them, and not for the survival of the species, as they may fool you to believe, for if they had the choice between the two few of them will choose the species as this is secondary to them.

No hero, heroine, God or Goddess were ever worshipped without their tools being intact and even the Aphrodite of Milos was incidentally preserved armless but intact. Ever wondered if she would attract as many admirers if only the head or feet were preserved? I hold that not to be the case, and I venture to say that if the head and the feet were taken out, as in the case of the Belvedere Torso, we will still find her beautiful. Why is that? It is because she would still be intact. This is ingrained in us.

Thus, the god or gods of men are but gods of men; they are men. Even when they honour goddesses, you will still find an Amun-Ra ruling over Amunet, a Zeus over Hera; I will spare you the list of the who is who of the other religions as the principle stands.

It seems to me that no human wants to worship what he or she deems to be a lesser being, no matter the material from which the divinity is made, yet they do.

Markers

Sometimes an offensive word roars more than the thunder

A frail tulip that blooms in a time of cold weather gives more hope than the most prosperous springs

A candle shining in the darkness seems brighter than thousands of suns

A smile in time, to an overwhelmed heart, gives more wealth than all the ephemeral gifts of the begging rich who tax us through a backhanded voice

A house made of wood holds more love than all the love we believe exists in the hearts in distress

On arid fields are born plants that one would believe are made of wood, if one does not see their tears made of morning dew

The silence of the stars speaks louder than all of the cries of the crowds in turmoil

The colour of dawn proceeding the horizon tells of the world better than all the books of history and says more truths than all the loose tongues of thoughts under the weight of shackles

The sunset paints the landscape with the colour of silence and the verve of patience next to the impertinence of madness

The waves with softness on the skin of love we know to be sovereign

On Failure and Arrogance

Some people are so used to having doors held open for them that they don't see gratitude, nor do they feel the need to bow to it, if they ever do, when it comes their way. Yet, gratitude comes back and they, still engulfed in their arrogance, call it a lost opportunity. Blind as they are to its apparent humble form, they may never know the reason for their failures; they continue seeing open doors not realizing that they lead to shutting gates.

On Discrimination's Impact

Discrimination, as abhorrent as it is, does not stop people from socially rising up, it is only, and this is part of its deep sedating psychological impact, when they believe that it does that it actually does.

The social improvement of the discriminated against is noted to their credit as they pushed for change despite the negative odds.

Light in the Dark

If you see through the candle mesh
You will see through the thickest night
A flame burning inside out; nothing around but your recurring inner light
You can't account for the illumination in the dark

When you perceive the promise of the spark
The birth of you in an eternity of impossible starts

You will remember that first sight of her walking in your life
The questions in your soul crashing the firmness of your despair
The vision of a distant, yet impactful pair
The hunger of a satisfied mind
The commencing of the unanticipated strife
The urge to know that which you think you know

The answer to the question you never asked
To find yourself is to find her in the blinding night

Ask the air to seek her in the Aether
It will race, come back, find the shy smile in the pleasant wind touching her hair
The grace of her pause next to the fleeing stars in envy of her beautiful weather
The summer of her sudden turns
The piercing heart that burns
With no flames, but with delight

The East vanquished by her rising suns
Two blue eyes tempering the fire of the Quasars
The secret of her essence is not knowing that she is the source and the light

Echoing in the depth of the hoping heart

To do what is right, not to be the thief of a granted love
In honesty to find the fleeting dove

To endure like the present; eternally remain as life's constant core
To last longer than the strongest metal or ore

Yes, call onto the moon to fetch an equivalent of her goodwill, it will vainly attempt to replicate the crescent of her delicious smile

Eclipsed, will be its rising state
Watch the stars as they imitate
The halo of her mind unseen
The vapour of the ocean, a mist of the dream dying to be real

If you see through the candle mesh
You will see through the thickest night

You may recognize the elements
You may recollect

A flame burning inside out; nothing around but a recurring inner light

On Thinking

As libraries used to be places where books were found, brains were places where individuals used to go to think, that is before communal warping messed them up.

To Every Author, in Sympathy

As I finished the book, I heard a voice that said to me, "No one has ever written such beautiful words!" I turned around, grabbed a cup of water and threw it at the face looking at me in the mirror. "Good-for-nothing. You want to bring me down to lowest of the low! I am not going to succumb to your chains of complacency!" I said to him.
Yet, the figure that was mine kept smiling.

It Will

It will pass, for life cares not for regrets

It favours those of its infants who of its darkness fashion lights

It will get better for it was not as good in your perception as the moment when you started regretting it

You will surpass it for you have endured it so far and you have not yet given up

You will heal, but you will not forget because a lesson forgotten is a lesson unlearned

A pain receding is an impact measured; an awareness gained

You will smile again for your spirit is broken but is not shattered. Otherwise, you would have had your pulse muted

You must know by now that the secret to surviving is not dying, though death hides in different manners

Fear to the coward is a treacherous companion; a hostage to terror in the hands of his worst enemies,

To the brave, fear is an unnecessary burden, but in light doses a welcome sense of caution; she plows through the night as darkness is conquered

The night is but the day rendered invisible

He who understands must improve for ignorance is a stagnant matter

Like death it shares the same constant; a consolidation of failures

It will pass for like everything else that is a slave to time, it must pause

In space there is a sense of redemption, but in time there are good memories

Of all that matters you are now the holder, the storyteller

In the darkness you carry a light of those of whom you had the privilege of being a companion,

Don't be shortsighted

You are a reflection of light to the others; the measure of endurance

Falter not for if you do, so does the light

And if you break it, then you have renegaded the gift of a lifetime

It is your turn, of darkness lights to fashion

It is Not Always Black and White

The sun that pales the moon also gives life to our planet.

On What You Could Be

If nature made you good looking or beautiful, remember that at least in your personality there is always much improvement to be done.

If nature made you plain looking, know then, that the middle ground is where we all must meet

If you believe that you were not endowed with beauty or plainness, then remember that those who believe that they have much to attain are endowed, if they exercise themselves, with creativity unmatched.

If none of the above applies to you, then know that you are the "all else" variable, the essence of life resides in you and nothing can break you. You are the way the rest of us don't how to be and yet you are still around, and if there ever was a miracle, then it is you; whether you know it or not is irrelevant, you are the exception; an inspiration.

If and When

If and when the stars come crushing on the solid surface of your thoughts,
Watch for and keep the rubble as the pieces will come back together

If and when the seas flood the shores of your eyes,
The receding waters will reveal the hidden treasures you never suspected in you existed
Watch for the vultures bent on keeping you down

If and when by your friends you are deserted,
Remember that the sand of time to you has provided its measuring resource,

An endless flow; there is no need to turn back the clock as for you it flows in all directions

If and when the Gods their powerless venting towards you they send their senseless chanting,
Care to keep asking the logical questions for evidence will shames them to the recesses of nonexistence

Bear the resolution of the human child facing the odds and surviving

The hope and good will of the old attempting to continue to walk

If and when the beasts push you into a corner,
Remember it for what it is; the edge of a cliff is for both equally dangerous
In your despair step not over a rose
For if you make it through, it is it that you need not to become a monster

If and when the ruffians their stories about you spread,
Let them spend their only resource,
Muted, the fatherless parrot is but a bird in extinction and so the dodo never made it

If and when the world seems crowded,
Try loneliness for a short while for it will surely fill your existence

When and if the world to you seems expensive, may I suggest you try the heavens and put your gaze on the ocean

And when death comes, to understand that fading is also to the sun and the galaxies related,
Look at the world, if you can, with observation and note that which you see for dying is a onetime occurrence,

To forget your grievances, as when you are asleep or in the darkness, for the light in you never surrenders

Rise your eyes up to see the heavens and the ocean

Ideals and Reality

In a fight between our ideals and reality, the module of reality tends to win, but our ideals once reinforced and no longer surprised tend to kick reality's derriere.

The Meaning of Life

On the planet X0281, when a person is about to enter adulthood, the first question he or she is asked in front of their peers is "Why have you decided to be born?" When he or she reaches mid-life he or she is again put on the stand and asked, "Why have you decided to continue to live?"

When reaching the age of retirement, he or she is asked, "what do you think made you endure?" To the three questions the boy as the man, the girl as the woman to themselves must answer, for if he or she does not have a response that person is deemed lacking awareness of their life, and as such, this is taken as a strong indication that this person never lived.

On Goodwill

The world without goodwill is like being on Earth and seeing the reflection of the Sun on the moon but without being able to see the glorious star that lights it; you only see the pale Moon.

On Love

If you listen carefully you will hear a symphony of light being played, it is that of you and your partner. It is also called love.

An Intuition

Out of the ashes of time, the sun rises and the earth and moon seem to smile

Towers of steep and sharp in the highest points show their faceless peaks

The birds greet the invisible air, they swim in the Aether
In the distance, behind the clouds, giants beat their drums
Rain drops from the depth of the sky fall

Invisible to reasons are the longings of the heart

Of the guts of artist is born an art

Ancient ways leading to ancient waves make the sea alight
Charms ingrained in women and men sift life through the night

Children walk and to silent tunes in the streets start to dance

They jump and easily bounce over the adults made fencc

To whom and why does the sun send light and sparks?

A blind man follows a dog following a scent

She flutters her angelic wings, makes a pause, and smiles

Her intrepid dress in the air flies

His face in his darkness is alight; he knows she is there for him to stay

Sun and moon, stars and essence, lighthouses and ships, love and heart; the one to the other showing the way

Far from the towers of kings and paupers' gates they found their light in the spark

In an endless embrace their course is set

A guitar finding its strings

A song it's wings

Order finally listening to Grace

The mind to its pace

Freedom ashamed, mindful of its walls and gates

Emptiness of void endlessly satiated

War of itself repudiated

Contrast and sameness one under the blinding light

Just like hunger and glut in the one endless night

You must know to know as in you must live to grow

If you don't, stagnation is the colour of the crow

As all that is lost must have been

All that is no more must somewhat have been seen

Nothing is out of life even impotent death

She flutters her wings, makes a pause, and smiles

Her intrepid dress in the air a flute to play

His face in his darkness is alight; he knows she is there for him to stay

ABOUT THE AUTHOR

Lamine Pearlheart is an avid reader and, as far as he remembers, he always had a great appreciation for literature, history, philosophy, poetry, and enjoys long walks as a meditation form.

One of his chief interests is the understanding of the human experience in its multidimensional aspects as is apparent in his books.

He also has a passion for languages; he speaks English, French, German, Spanish and Portuguese.

The author is currently working on his first novel.

www.ingramcontent.com/pod-product-compliance
Ingram Content Group UK Ltd.
Pitfield, Milton Keynes, MK11 3LW, UK
UKHW040009200726
13854UKWH00001B/108

9 781999 575106